This notebook belongs to:

Enjoying this notebook?

Please leave a review because we would love to hear your feedback, opinions, and advice to create better products and services for you! Also, we want to know how you creatively use your notebooks and journals.

Thank you so much for your support. **You are greatly appreciated!**

Joyful Journals ☺

Made in the USA
Coppell, TX
05 April 2020